The Art Of Poetry

A Collection of Poems

Sourav Kumar

© **Sourav Kumar 2023**

All rights reserved

All rights reserved by author. No part of this publication may be reproduced, stored in a retrieval system or transmitted in any form or by any means, electronic, mechanical, photocopying, recording or otherwise, without the prior permission of the author.

Although every precaution has been taken to verify the accuracy of the information contained herein, the author and publisher assume no responsibility for any errors or omissions. No liability is assumed for damages that may result from the use of information contained within.

First Published in March 2023

ISBN: 978-93-5741-236-0

BLUEROSE PUBLISHERS

www.BlueRoseONE.com

info@bluerosepublishers.com

+91 8882 898 898

Cover Design:

Yash

Typographic Design:

Tanya Raj Upadhyay

Distributed by: BlueRose, Amazon, Flipkart

About the Book

This book is a collection of poems. All the poems are well composed with rhyming words and with a moral value. There are twenty six poems inside. The themes of the poems are based on nature, social issues, humanity and natural occurrences.

This book is a mirror of current social affairs. I am sure the readers would realize the feeling of patriotism and humanism after this book. The use of 'Figure of Speech' is one more remarkable point in this book. To create interest while reading, 'alliteration is used majorly. Moreover, The 'Titles' of the poems will persuade the readers to go through the whole writing.

Foreword

As a writer I wanted to raise all the social concerns through my writings. That's why I used my words as a weapon to motivate, to inspire, to show concern and to draw the attention of people towards disbeliefs and the real value of human life.

To bring a revolution in the society on the basis of natural and social reformation, I penned down this book. In my opinion we cannot control the increasing malpractice in society until we change our thoughts. The upcoming generations can be motivated and inspired so that they will not harm the nature and can be understood the value of resources.

Preface

As we know that literature plays a crucial role in forming the character of humans and in making aware the people towards their cultures, traditions, civilizations and ancestors.

Writing is a medium to put on one's thoughts and ideas before the society. So I, here, urge and push forward to become an avid reader first and, then, to ponder over ideas and lessons a reader gets on reading a book.

The preface of this book is to awaken the tired souls and to inspire the readers towards their goals by fighting against the obstacles, that come the way, are considered as the stairs to success.

Contents

The Obstacle

I come in each
And every life,
Not only once, but
Many and many times.

I knock at their lives
To make them aware of their skills.
Being a dissenter from every point, I boost
Them up for the coming miles.

Prevailing on their ways
Like the stairs that lead them
To the success, I dare to create
An upheaval against their waves.

My intention is not to deter
Their efforts and attempts,
But, to assess their parameters.
Whenever I am faced,
The target is chased.

Working like a chisel,
As they are so kind.
I weed out the roughage
From their mind.

Awaking their snorting souls,
I stimulate them, to do
Something new,
That takes place very few
To take them to their goals.

Standing before them
Like a barrier, I drive them on
To accept my summons
As soon as they can.
I'd come again and again.

The Dying Nature

A long ago, large and luring meadows,
And sparkling streams in the shining sun
When they flowed down mountains with
Frosted ice reflected the beauty of the nature
By casting their shadows.

The woods, where wild beasts would dwell,
Have been taken out with high towers.
Shallow waters remain present either in rivers
Or in wells,
As without mountains there are no showers.

Chirping and conveying a message of unity,
A few flocks of birds flew in the air.

Hunted and losing their habitats,
Some species lost their existence.
And they left the sky bare.

Bearing excess modifications, the nature
Yells and shows its fury by creating crises
Think, learn from its past horrified scenes
And be cautioned or get ready to owe prices.

The Life Of Farmers

Wandering through farms, they weed and
Watch their yields from dim dawn.
Till dusk they wait and wait for waters in the
Form of rain sitting in a nearby lawn.

Not only in day, but also in dreading dark,
They wake leaving their homes.
Unaware of the hidden enemies, they sleep with
Short snorts in their granaries, hearing the
Melodies sung by the larks.

Oh, what a worse consequence they got!
Dried and deserted with droughts, the lands

Look like deserts, whereas in some regions
The farms with full of flowing waters look like
Lakes in which they may sail boats.

The hard labour and the gracious of getting
Goods got washed away with a whip
Of the nature.
Shocked, silent and stunned, they stare at their
Farms hoping for prosperity in future.

Seasons

Foliage to flora and fauna, I bring;
When they look like skeletons.
With cold and whirling breeze;
I rejuvenate them to flower
Whose nectar may be sucked by bees.
I am known as spring.

In the shining and scorching Sun;
I make men move to their mansions
In the month of May.
To take a draught of water, they run;
From the basins of brooks to the bays.
I am known as summer.

With thunders and lightings my journey
Begins when summer lasts.
I quench the thirst of the Earth by irrigating
The crops from one farm to another farm.
The brooks get brimmed and begin to flow
Fast.
Lands get rid of drought, but I don't harm.
I am called monsoon.

Slashing the length of day, I elongate the
Night.
Not in a straight way, but all around the layer
Of smog looks quite white.
Shivering and suffering from cold with
Curtailing celsius, creatures become silent.
It all happens when I become violent.
I am known as winter.

A Mart

Wow! How trimmed, glamorous and crowded

Shops there are!
Not for a little area, but they are seen, in a
Straight queue, for so far.

It's a mart which bears the delights of one's
Children and the needs of his life.
He may get here everything whether it is a
Heavy thing like a car or a light thing like
A knife.

Rushing in or out at the shops, he may see
So many recondite faces.
Some keep bargaining for their rapturous Items,
But some of them keep moving, carrying the briefcases.
At a marketplace, this type of scene is without
Any fee.

A source of livelihood, it is considered,
As many people become self-employed.
To consummate the needs of people,
From here, door to door, things are delivered.

Humanism - A Religion

I wish there were merely one religion,
All in one, which is humanism.
No one would create rage nor lives would be
Sacrificed suppressing a secluded race
And all the world would hang on to unionism.

Religions don't teach us to create hostility,
But they cause some bad practices like
Discrimination, apartheid and partition of people
In various races.
Humans are divided across the world
Into many faces.

No religion is greater than humanism
As all the sacred books are written on the
Same theme.
People bow their heads in front of worship
Places, but the temple of humanism is
Supreme.

Just be up to unite the world in a single
Religion.
One day, it would be ensued in all the
Regions.

Crime and Corruption

Alas! Alas!
With the newspapers reviews and from the
Gossiping among people who get together.
Someone may get extremely shocking and
Horrified news that is beyond rather.

Nowadays, murder, robbery, abduction and
Scam are the words which carry the headlines
Of journalism.
These crimes don't take place seldom,
But day to day, they are beheading humanism.

Alas! Alas!
It is the world of crime where there is no
Security of lives even not of those who are
The creators.
O Yes! Its violent flames don't recognise
Whether someone is a predator or a mediator or a
creator.

How! How is it flourishing?
This is because it is assisted by the system,
Which is supposed to curb it, known as bureaucracy.
Both crime and corruption are allied together
And they are chopping up democracy.

Don't...don't keep these occupations on.
They eat our own.

Decisions Must Be Own

Not only once but many and many times,
We all need to make decisions.
Sometimes others advise us as there come
Several situations which creates confusions--
What to do, how to do and when to do.

Listening to others' advice is a good habit.
But, the advices merely assist in making
Decisions since they're just their opinions.
Instead of listening to our hearts, if we directly
Take them as decisions, they may move us
Back to the pavilion.

Those all who are wearing crowns.
They decide on their own.

I Love my India

The land of gods! It is the country where
Many deities took incarnation as human beings.
They ever born with the name of 'RAM'
Or ever born with the name of 'SITA'.
We may tune their hymns by reading
The sacred book known as 'GITA'.
And all the dramas occurring here are played
By the almighty 'SHIVA' who is worshiped
In the form of 'SHIVLING'.

It is known as a secular country
As all the religions are having equal
Fundamental rights and duties.
It is full of diversity in the fields of cultures
and languages which enhance its beauty.

With the bloods of martyrs, its map is painted.
And still the soldiers are restless to sacrifice
Their lives to save its pride.
Neither they worry for their sons nor for their brides.
That is why, the enemies are getting fainted.

It is the land where people play 'DANDIYA'
SO, I love my 'INDIA'

The Journey Of Life

From the day when we born,
The journey of our lives lifts.
Through so many hurdles, it shifts.
By facing them, it is adorned.

Day to day, it passes
And leaves new pictures behind for our
Memories.
Some of them are full of entertainment.
But, some bear the pains of clashes
Which takes the edge off its excitement.

On its path, we ever get mirth
Or ever get gloom.
But, each moment has its own worth.
Since the spell of life is finite,
So, it keeps its journey on till it gets doomed.

Let's enjoy the journey of our lives
Carrying out all the liabilities.
As we all are traveling to a single destination.
So, there is no need for hostility.

A Real Player

Many and many games, all the people play,
Throughout their lives.
They ever lose since they delay
While chasing the goal or they ever get triumph
Because they dive
Upon the target at the right time.

Like storms, there several situations,
Come before a player, which deter him
And divert his appropriate direction.
By facing them, he loses his patience
And his aspirations become dim.
That is why he gets compelled to give up.

Whereas, a real player accepts them
Assuming that they are parts of the game.
With his self confidence, he waits for his turn,
But, never loses his patience and does not let
His aspirations and expectations burn.

Till the last moment he keeps his hope alive,
Without Knowing the consequence whether
He would succeed or lose. All the games he
Plays in the same manner in all the weathers.

I wish I were a star

Of course! To become a star, each and every
Adolescents keep dreaming.
They ever imitate the actions acted by their
Favorite stars or keep the roles played by
Them clinging to their memories which remain
Brimming.

Like them, I too was ever an adolescent and
Would dream the same.
I wished to become a star so that my parents could feel
proud of me and I could get Unique fame.

So many characters I preferred
To act on them. But, I was unaware of my
Skills and couldn't decide what to do.
So, one to another they were referred.

Once, I got an opportunity to become aware
Of my talents.
Do you want to know?
What was the opportunity?
That was my writing skills.
Of course! As I initiated to write poetry,
I clutched it and became violent.
Of becoming a star, I'm on the brink.

Road-Accident

How glad the man was!
For his baby, he was purchasing sweets,
And for his spouse, some cosmetics despite
Having the droplets of pouring sweats.

In a hurry, he wished to reach his door
So that he might enjoy his family life
By playing romance with his wife
And his little one couldn't wait anymore.

Ah, How unfortunate he was!
By a rashly moving van, he was run over
While crossing the road and all his articles

Bearing the prosperity of his family flung off
Into the adjoining lawn.

For a relishing dish the moment left his little one
waiting.
And ready for romance his wife remained getting.
Now, Who will look after them?
Their lives have become damn..

The poem appeals not to drive fast.
It leads one's life to the last.

Self-Confidence

Maybe! One has lost everything,
And is waiting for his last decline.
His self confidence, the same time, steals
Through his ears saying, " I'd let you
Remain anxious for nothing."
For all his woes, it acts as balms to heal.

Deterred with his failures, he sits down
And is about to abandon his endeavors.
Then, he's assisted by his self confidence
With the words, 'Once More', Come into lawn
With all your might and ever done labour.

Criticized by them, he roams, here and there,
To look for a new cottage to shelter himself.
At once, his self confidence holds his hands
And tells him to stay at the place, from where
He got criticisms, so that he could get
Triumph over them and, of admiration, could play his
wands.

O YES!
It's his self confidence which empowers him
To withstand all the critics and press on
His strives until he succeeds with his ambition
And his bout is considered gone.

A Poor Person

Alas! Being a hard worker, yet he remains
Deprived of his drowning dreams.
He, though, works a lot, but cheers himself up
By remaining without creased costumes and
Consummating his children with crimson creams.

Late he lays in bed and gets up before the sun,
From the dimming dawn
To the dark and dreadful dusk,
He wanders up and down across the town
So that he could get a brimming bowl of buns.

Alas! Being aware of his economical status,
Yet he glares and gazes at a convent and wishes
He were prodigal instead of a poor person
So that his children could get that status
With demanded and delicious dishes.

Like a versatile, he persuades himself
To carry out the toughest and tiring tasks,
With any consequence, whether he might
Fall ill or, in the sun, may bask.

I'm proud to be a teacher

Oh, What a character I play!
The most liable job towards our nation,
By bestowing the budding stars a lot of beneficial
notions,
Since they're considered soft clays.

Like the soldiers with the sophisticated weapons,
I too serve the motherland, but with the pens.
Hence, the profession is assumed not only as a job but
also as a kind of service.
Being aware of it, I wish to keep on.

Representing myself, I'm recognized,
With my behaviours as well as with my actions,
Which must be pursued so that they might get
sanctioned.

Oh, what a character I play!
So many roles are played across the earth,
But no one is having the dignity like teaching,
And its debt can't be repaid at any worth.

Parents are guardians of mere their children,
But, I'm considered the guardian of plenty of children.
So, I'm proud to be a teacher,
As I'm having so many features.

Health is wealth

Of course! One retains his devotion
Towards his family,
By impersonating his character to be a guardian
Not only gladly but also lamely.

Working more hours than it is required,
Though, he earns a lot for his wealth,
But, can't hang on to his own health
That is considered as natural wealth.

The worst it takes him to,
As he becomes paraplegic
To walk a few miles,

Yet he presses on his assignments with overtime.
Hence, to take rest he is prescribed
Due to piles.

33

The hard labour gets washed away
Since he's to pay a worth
With all his wealths which is acquired with it,
as he goes under treatment
To have his natural wealth.

I ever wonder we run motors or they run us,
Within my mind it has created a fuss.

At the Age Of Seventeenth

The first phase, I's traveling in,
Of getting a youth, to win
The heart of a lass after passing
The age which was seventeenth.

To replenish the desire of my heart,
The beauty of a girl, caught my sight,
With her luring figure and short skirt,
And made me mad for all the nights.

The mere purpose she became,
Of my presence in the class.
As we were in the same standard,

That was the same.
I wished to the hours not to pass.

All the endeavours and ventures, I made,
Like gazing at and following her, to own her, but didn't dare to propose her,
Because of her rebuff, I was afraid.

By doing so, I just tried to retain
The hope of getting her love as without it
Hard those moments'd have been for me.
That is why the efforts I made went in vain.

A Hero Inside you

Hey, what are you looking for?
'A hero'! just dare to take a glimpse
Inside yourself, 'A hero' you would find.
Then no need to look for more.

A lots of characters you 're assigned
Throughout your life, by playing them
With full fidelity and culpability,
'A hero', you'd be recognised.

Hey, what are you looking for?
'A hero'! maybe you get him,
But he'd not impersonate your characters
Since merely you 're the best for.
As to me it seems.

Having the possessing attitude,
Hard it 'd be and like a nightmare
To become 'A hero', Unless you
Rush out to procure an individual aptitude.

Until you become aware of it
In which stream 'A hero' you are.
Just you'd be a spectator of 'A hero'
As your visions'd remain so far.

Winning and Losing

Winning and losing', the two sides of a game
And remain together both of them.
May not take place one without another,
Having such an assumption is beyond rather.

The mirth of winning is delectable
Since with a lot of patience it is hugged.
But, confronting the possessing lackness,
The moments of losing are assessable.

One, by whom losing is faced,
Keeps making his strives at a strike.

By the same, at once, the goal of winning is chased,
And, by then, he wishes to get alike.

'Winning and losing' the two sides of a game
And remain together both of them.
The gracious for getting goal losing towers,
If it lacks, winning never hovers.

A lesson from Lincoln's life losing rewards,
Instead of bestowing winning awards.
May not take place one without another,
Having such an assumption is beyond rather.

Life Without Love

It's life-- a pouch of liabilities and excitements,
But, without love there is no entertainment.

It is merely an idol like a doll
And love is considered as its soul.

It remains deprived of relishing shade
At the place where love is dead.

Might be bargained everything at a worth
Whereas, love is honorary across the earth.

Though an ocean of love it is, but thirsty,
Terrified by the flaming violence,
To spill out its waves and tides
That prefers to retain silence.

Need to be coloured the desert of life
With the foliage of affections.
Instead of having the pride
With a lot of fake passions.

This poem appeals either to burn or to bury
The words like wrath, vanity and fury.

The Passing Time

Hold me! Hold me!
I am bound for a definite deed,
Which must be done with me.
As it keeps your heed.

Some just let me pass in vain
And lost their existence.
If you withstand my pain,
You 'd surely retain with your life's persistence.

So many opportunities, I bear
Into my pouch,
Just need to be searched it into
And you must pick up the best

Out of them with which
You could become your own seer.

Hold me! Hold me!
For you I bear even a lot of lessons,
That remains left behind me.
Up they would boost you to realize
My significance for the waiting sessions.

It 's my earnest desire to put
The wreath of your mirth on.
As I want to adorn myself
With it before getting gone.

I would return never,
To say you anything more.
So, do something times four
And let me cling to your memories forever.

The Mistake

Making me is a manifestation,
Towards your trails,
That you're strolling on
A way of amelioration.

Prevailing in your nature,
I compel you, to ponder
A little more, to enhance your own features
That embellishes your attempts like a wonder.

To present you for your experience book,
I take place, from your childhood to your old stage, to
adorn it with a fabulous look.

Why you feel shame
Whenever I knock at your attempts.
I provoke you to remind your next steps
Which would give you unique fame.

Through my series, each and every creation
Has shifted. By getting the strokes
Of my hammer, up they have been boosted.

Let me do my own duty,
Like a caretaker of your efforts, to take them
Off to the apex of their beauty

A Lullaby of Old Couples

Do you ever remember?
Those days, when we'd replenish you
With the stationeries,
To make you enrolled in a missionary.

We'd march to mart on bare foot,
To deplete the expense of money,
So that your outfit could be
Adorned with the shining boots,
And while taking supper you
Could taste the honey.

Carrying out your visions,
To make you glad along with ourselves,
We'd withstand the shylocks
Whether it's scorching summer,
Chilled winter or any season.

Come and make us put the new costumes on.
As we have become old couples
With the numerous wrinkles.
So, like your spouse, we're unable to twinkle.

It's expected, by each and every like us,
That they'd be sheltered at their own homes,
Instead of throwing in old age homes.

Like maids we'd serve your wife
During her pregnancy period,
Instead of enhancing your burdens,
We'd look after a new life.

Having a wish before getting buried, we hope
You feed us with your hands.
As it's time to tune the hymns
Of the motherland.

The Struggle

It is my prediction,
That you'd be familiar
With me. As I am the pedestal
Of your future's constitution.

I'm like a furnace,
That scorches you to mend
Your future, that keeps you
Away from the coming menace.

Irrigating you with my warmth,
I bestow you a chance,
In each and every field,
That gives you the strength to enhance
Your own yield.

Accompanying you throughout
Your journey,
I attempt to take you off to a great ceremony.

Never forget to carry me on.
If you do so, your visions would not be your own.

I'm as bitter as a 'chili',
For those who honor you
With the word like 'silly'.

My friend, let me mingle
With your gingle.
I'd not let you remain single.
I'd not let you.

The Marriage Ceremony

Oh, how momentous the day is!
The day when a maiden girl becomes bride,
And she persuades herself to begin a new
Journey.
Till this day, her father cherishes and
Nourishes her since she is her pride.
For his daughter's delight, he hides his tears
While arranging the marriage ceremony.

It is truly said that women renounce
At all the stages.
From their parental homes after marriage,
At first, they get detached.
And here at the ceremony,

A woman, who is the mother of the
Bride, waits for the last phase
Of the marriage ceremony as her daughter,
Who is her heartbeat, with a peculiar
Family, gets attached.

But, what about the bridegroom! A marriage
Ceremony is abridged without him.
A young boy, who is unaware of liabilities,
Becomes liable forever.
By then, he gives his mischief up and begins
To do harder labour than ever.

www.ingramcontent.com/pod-product-compliance
Lightning Source LLC
La Vergne TN
LVHW051311200726

843510LV00010B/1365